Original title:
Oasis of Tranquility

Copyright © 2025 Creative Arts Management OÜ
All rights reserved.

Author: Clara Whitfield
ISBN HARDBACK: 978-1-80581-592-1
ISBN PAPERBACK: 978-1-80581-119-0
ISBN EBOOK: 978-1-80581-592-1

The Gentle Whisper

In a world that's loud, I seek my space,
Where silence wears a friendly face.
A butterfly once told a joke,
And all the cacti simply broke.

Refuge from the Roar

When life's a circus, I grab my chair,
With popcorn kernels floating in the air.
Sunshine giggles, shadows dance,
While wise old turtles plot their chance.

The Comforting Haven

Here, the breeze shares secrets well,
Of how to laugh and how to dwell.
Squirrels plot with acorn plans,
In comfy corners, they spark some prans.

Meditation's Edge

In stillness, frogs recite some rhymes,
While crickets string their chime-in-climbs.
A sage with glasses sips on tea,
And claims the wind is made of glee.

Shimmering Stillness

The pond reflects a silly duck,
Wearing sunglasses, what a luck!
It quacks in joy, a splashy show,
While frogs join in with a ribbit glow.

Breezes dance with a cheeky grin,
As flowers swish, they all spin in.
Even the rocks seem to giggle loud,
In this calm space, they feel so proud.

Lullaby of Nature

Chatty squirrels play peek-a-boo,
While sleepy leaves hum a gentle tune.
A turtle yawns, stretching with flair,
As bees buzz softly, without a care.

The grass takes a nap, its blades all stacked,
While critters gather, their laughter unpacked.
A snail drags behind, slow as can be,
In this calming world, they all feel free.

Reflection Pool

A mirror of giggles beneath the trees,
Where fish swim in rhythm, dancing with ease.
A lone manatee joins the playful crowd,
With a flip of a fin, it feels so proud.

The clouds overhead play tag with the sun,
While a frog with a hat thinks it's all just fun.
Ripples spread wide, laughter on display,
In this calm pool, joy leads the way.

Sweet Repose

Pillows of moss invite a brief nap,
Where bumblebees snore in a fuzzy flap.
A raccoon juggles while dreaming away,
In the stillness, all worries decay.

The sunset giggles as colors collide,
Painting the sky, a canvas wide.
The quiet chuckle of night creeps in slow,
Bringing peace wrapped in a warm, funny glow.

Tranquil Reflections

In a pond that shines like glass,
A frog leaps in, oh what a splash!
He laughs at fish that swim in fear,
While water lilies cheer, it's clear!

With dragonflies that zoom around,
Their tiny wings make quite a sound.
They gossip 'bout the clouds up high,
While robins sing and giggle by.

Respite in the Meadow

In fields where flowers play and dance,
A bee gets lost in a flower trance.
He bumps a bloom, it giggles loud,
And soon a whole bunch joins the crowd!

A squirrel with acorns in his paws,
Thinks he's the king, with royal laws.
He tells the ants, "Forage in style!"
They nod and march in single file.

Serene Skies Above

Clouds drift by, they look like sheep,
As seagulls caw and dive, then leap.
A sunbeam tickles all below,
While skinny shadows start to glow.

An eagle soars, a funny sight,
He clucks and flaps in pure delight.
With flapping wings and wild ballet,
He dances through the skies all day.

Cradle of the Quiet Mind

A hammock sways beneath a tree,
Where thoughts float by, all wild and free.
A raccoon peeks, with mischief in his eyes,
As squirrels plan their heist, oh what a surprise!

And in this calm, the laughter flows,
For nature's jokes are quite the prose.
A chipmunk squeaks a witty line,
While daisies nod, it's all divine!

Twilight's Embrace

In the dusk where shadows play,
The squirrels dance, hip-hop ballet.
Crickets chirp their nightly joke,
While fireflies wear their tiny cloak.

A cactus with its prickly grin,
Says, 'Chill out, let the fun begin!'
The moon winks down with a cheesy smile,
As we unwind and rest a while.

The Quietude Factors

A turtle in a sunlit sprawl,
Dreams of racing, though it's slow and small.
A wise old owl hoots a pun,
'Who needs haste? Let's just have fun!'

The pond reflects a jolly frog,
Croaking tunes as he logs his blog.
Amidst the trees that sway and bend,
The laughter here will never end.

Nature's Gentle Lullaby

The babbling brook tells silly tales,
Of frogs that wear their tiny veils.
A gentle breeze carries a tune,
As if the daisies dance to the moon.

A sleepy bear yawns with a sigh,
Comfy in clouds way up high.
While starry giggles grace the night,
Nature's humor takes flight.

The Peaceful Grove

In the grove where giggles bloom,
A hedgehog rolls, spreading good mood.
Branches sway in a funky beat,
As raccoons gather for a treat.

The sunlight peeks, a playful spy,
Tickling leaves as the wind floats by.
The harmony of joyy we weave,
In laughter's glow, we all believe.

Sacred Silence

In a garden whose weeds just won't quit,
A gnome danced with moves that were quite a hit.
The cactus gave input, quite sharp with his words,
While flowers murmured in laughter with birds.

Beneath the bright sun, a snail made a race,
Claiming victory with elegant grace.
A breeze, like a joke, caught everyone off guard,
While crickets formed bands in the backyard yard.

Enchanted Serenity

At dusk, the bunnies held a tea bash,
With cookies and tales that made all of us crash.
The hedgehog wore slippers, so fuzzy and cute,
While toads played the lute in their finest pursuit.

In the shade, a turtle played cards with his pals,
Betting acorns and shells, like rich little gals.
The sun winked, as if sharing a secret delight,
While fireflies twinkled, a spark in the night.

Clouds of Contentment

A cat on a cloud with a grin so wide,
Catnip was flowing like it was a tide.
The mice were on strike, with a union so bold,
Trading tales of cheese that were thoroughly told.

Pigeons debated their fashion, well-dressed,
Arguing feathers that fluffed up their best.
While squirrels held meetings, tossing out terms,
On how to store nuts in the midst of all germs.

Waves of Elysium

In a pond, frogs planned their day at the mall,
While fish cast their votes for the best swimming hall.
The ducks quacked their gossip, a splashy affair,
While turtles just lounged without a single care.

Seagulls overhead traded stories of snacks,
As crabs on the shoreline formed their own hacks.
With laughter and splashes, the day rolled along,
A medley of chaos where all felt they belonged.

Echoes of Harmony

In the midst of a stormy day,
A rubber duck sashays away.
It quacks in time, a silly tune,
While dancing 'neath a disco moon.

The cactus wears a party hat,
A playful cat joins in just that.
They waltz on clouds, so fluffy and bright,
Two misfits lost in pure delight.

Seraphic Retreats

Two penguins nap on a sunlit rock,
While a wise-old owl conks with a clock.
Pancakes flip in the gentle breeze,
As squirrels serve tea with such great ease.

A comical frog in a tuxedo jumps,
While laughter erupts from tree-trunk chumps.
The shade will tickle your sunburnt nose,
As the breeze tells stories of giggles and woes.

Distant Murmurs of Solitude

A llama prances in bright pink shoes,
While clowns juggle rubbery snooze.
In the twilight glow, they spin and glide,
Each twist and turn, a wild ride.

The fireflies hold a glow-stick rave,
As a sleepy bear takes a cozy knave.
The whispers of laughter float through the air,
Creating a scene that's beyond compare.

The Quiet Glade

A squirrel in shades counts all the nuts,
While an owl shares jokes with silly cuts.
In stillness, the dance of the breezy trees,
Turns giggles to whispers, oh such decrees!

The moon chuckles down at the cat's ballet,
As crickets join in the oddest way.
In a peaceful nook, life's quirks unfold,
In laughter's embrace, the tales are told.

Harbor of Restful Dreams

In a boat of cheese, I softly drift,
With marshmallow clouds, my sweet little gift.
Sailing on ketchup, the waves start to sway,
I giggle at seagulls who steal fries away.

A hammock of spaghetti swings in the breeze,
While meatball stars dance with such goofy ease.
The sun wears sunscreen, all lathered and bright,
As I nap with a pickle, all snug for the night.

The Lullaby of Nature

Crickets sing songs in a jazzy parade,
Bugs in tuxedos, all finely displayed.
The trees sway and shimmy in sandy ballet,
While squirrels juggle acorns, a nutty soiree.

The moon pulls a prank, with bright cosmic beams,
Tickling the blossoms, waking up dreams.
With giggles of fireflies lighting the dark,
Nature's a comedian, a feathered spark!

Shadows of Serenity

In the corner, a shadow with mismatched socks,
Tells tales of an octopus that dances and mocks.
While daisies do yoga in their leafy attire,
The shadows throw parties, they're quite the choir.

A calm breeze whispers all secrets the night,
Whimsical wonders that tickle delight.
Dandelions float, making wishes on whims,
As laughter erupts from the sprightly old limbs.

Dreaming in Still Waters

Reflections of ducks wearing bright yellow hats,
Swim past my thoughts, oh how time just chats.
The lily pads giggle, all froggy and wise,
While turtles trade gossip under sapphire skies.

Water so calm, it's a mirror for dreams,
Dancing with moonbeams like little moonbeams.
As fish play charades, in bubbles they gleam,
I float on my raft, lost in this dream.

Gentle Ripples of Peace

In the pond, a frog jumps nice,
Sharing whispers, oh, no price.
The dragonflies dance, a wild charade,
While turtles laugh at the antics made.

A breeze tickles the tall green grass,
As squirrels gossip, this day will pass.
With giggles from the fish below,
Tickled fins in soft ebb and flow.

A Haven in the Desert

A cactus wearing a sunhat wide,
Waves 'hello' to the lizards that glide.
Sand dunes jump like a playful pup,
While a hungry bird's quirks erupt.

The sun laughs down with a golden grin,
As camels gossip, "Where've you been?"
Something's brewing, a mirage's tease,
Oh, just a joke in the summer breeze.

Breath of the Melodic Breeze

Whispers float on the scented air,
The wind makes hairdos everywhere.
A melodic tune from the trees up high,
Has chipmunks dancing, oh my, oh my!

Leaves clap hands as they twist and sway,
With songs to chase the clouds away.
A butterfly twirls in a bright ballet,
Leaving a trail of giggles today.

In the Heart of Stillness

A turtle dozes, dreams of flight,
While a snail's in a race, taking all night.
Stillness giggles with playful grace,
As shadows sneak to join the chase.

Fireflies blink like tiny stars,
Every blink just raises the bars.
Amidst the hush, the critters play,
Dancing joyfully as night claims the day.

Inner Sanctum

In a garden where the cacti play,
The bunnies hop in a comical way.
A turtle spills tea with a face so bright,
While birds share jokes, taking flight.

Here, the squirrels wear sunglasses cool,
Dancing on branches, breaking the rule.
A breeze tickles noses, laughter in the air,
As the hedgehogs joke, without a care.

The goldfish chuckle, floating with glee,
Painting their scales with hues of brie.
While daisies giggle, swaying their heads,
In this silly land where joy spreads.

So grab your teacup, let's sit and sip,
Join the fun on this whimsical trip.
With laughter and smiles, we find our bliss,
In a world where humor is hard to miss.

Harbor of Solace

Where the sunsets drip like ice cream cones,
And ducks wear hats, not made of bones.
The fish hold meetings, discussing the bait,
While crabs play checkers, it's never too late.

With wind chimes giggling and clouds in a race,
Silly shadows dance, hopping from place to place.
In this quirky bay, the jellyfish sing,
As seagulls play fetch, a most joyful fling.

Mermaids debate if they should wear shoes,
While starfish trade tales of their best fish snooze.
Down at the docks, the old otters joke,
As they juggle shells, sending giggles to smoke.

So come for the cheer, and leave all your care,
In this harbor of fun that's beyond compare.
With laughter that echoes and joy that won't cease,
We find our own rhythm, a giggly release.

Calm in the Chaos

In a world filled with clatter,
My cat thinks he's a king;
He struts like he owns the platter,
While I just laugh and cling.

A dog barks through the ruckus,
Chasing squirrels with wild glee;
While I sip my chamomile, thus,
Life seems a comedy spree.

Traffic jams can't confuse me,
With a snack and a good book;
Even in chaos I see,
Every page is a nook.

So here's to the madness,
With a wink and a grin;
Finding joy in the badness,
Let the laughs begin!

Ethereal Embrace

Clouds dance like silly socks,
In skies of faded blue;
Butterflies wear fuzzy frocks,
Waving as they bid adieu.

The leaves whisper sweet secrets,
To the gregarious trees;
Nature cracks jokes in snippets,
Tickling the buzzing bees.

Moonlight spills like warm honey,
On the pond that's aglow;
Frogs croak laughs, it's so funny,
Dancing 'round with a show.

The stars wink at the jesters,
Playing tag with the night;
In this realm of fun festers,
Every moment feels right!

Restore the Soul

In a hammock strung with dreams,
I sway like a pendulum;
Life is sweeter than it seems,
With a snack of bubblegum.

Turtles stroll in slow motion,
Fashioned in their own style;
Their lazy, charming notion,
Makes me giggle for a while.

The breeze sings a funny tune,
As I wiggle my toes free;
Each moment is a cartoon,
Of this life's merry spree.

With a wink to the sunbeam,
I dive into my cocoon;
Restoration's not a dream,
When laughter's the best boon!

Spheres of Stillness

Bubbles float like small planets,
   Caught in a gentle breeze;
  I chase them like a bandit,
Clutching snacks—oh, what a tease!

The goldfish swims with purpose,
    A little round buffoon;
  While flowers laugh in circus,
   Underneath the silly moon.

Time slows down, it whispers, "Hey,"
   As I munch on some cheese;
   In this quirky, fun array,
   Life's chaos turns to tease.

So let's giggle through the haze,
With routines turned on their head;
 Finding joy through silly ways,
  In stillness, laughter's spread!

Harmonious Hideaway

In a patch of green, I found my chair,
A squirrel demands I share my pear.
He dances around, a furry delight,
While I sip lemonade, under sunlight.

Birds chirp gossip about the moon,
And all the frogs sing a lazy tune.
I chuckle at bees that buzz too near,
While contemplating my fulfilling career.

A cat lazily catches a sunbeam's flight,
While I munch chips with newfound delight.
The breeze carries laughter, a fruity scent,
In this silly garden, my time is well spent.

So here's to the moments, so freely shared,
Where laughter and snacks show that no one cared.
Life's quirks make us smile, let's not pretend,
In this hideaway, the jokes never end.

Tranquil Horizons

At sunrise, I spot my neighbor's pug,
Who thinks he's a lion, with quite the shrug.
He snores under flowers, a majestic beast,\nIn a kingdom of grass, he claims the least.

Fish in nearby ponds give a shiny grin,
As I wave at ducks—they wave back, with a spin.
The sun winks down, a mischievous friend,
Spreading giggles until daylight's end.

Clouds float on by, with mops in tow,
Cleaning up troubles that bloom below.
While ants throw a party, a bustling crew,
Dancing on crumbs from last week's barbecue.

I sit on the porch, feeling smug and spry,
With a cat who insists on being my tie.
In this peaceful scene, we embrace the fun,
As laughter and snacks blend, two souls as one.

Essence of Equanimity

In a hammock strung between two trees,
I rock and roll with the buzzing bees.
They wonder what I'm doing with flair,
I tell them, 'Just hanging—a casual affair!'

The sun laughs bright, a spotlight above,
As I toss peanuts to a squirrel I love.
He catches them deftly, a talented chap,
And winks at me proudly, oh what a nap!

Clouds drift on by, like lazy balloons,
While frogs strike up their ribbiting tunes.
A tortoise thinks he'll win this race,
But I'm already napping, my favorite place.

In this soft realm, where weird things thrive,
The jokes and giggles keep us alive.
So if you seek calm with a dash of mirth,
Join in the laughter, explore the earth!

Tides of Serenity

Waves crash on shores, with a playful spree,
As crabs do the cha-cha with a splashy glee.
While seashells gossip about beach gossip,
I sip my coconut and let my worries drop.

Seagulls perform, with a squawky cheer,
One steals my sandwich—hey, that's not fair!
But laughter erupts from the sun-kissed crowd,
As we rally together, feeling proud.

The waves are a rhythm, a comical beat,
That makes even grumpy folks tap their feet.
Each splish and splash carries joy so free,
In this bizarre beach party, just you and me.

So here's to the tides that come and they go,
With humor that blossoms wherever we flow.
In these moments of joy, let's all take a dive,
As we surf on this wave, we feel so alive.

Nestled in the Green

In the heart of lush delight,
Where squirrels dance and take flight.
A cactus wearing a silly hat,
Sips lemonade while a bird chats.

The sun pops in for tea at dawn,
While grasshoppers show off their brawn.
They juggle acorns without a fuss,
As butterflies giggle, it's a must!

Even the flowers wear goofy grins,
While rabbits practice their silly spins.
A frog croaks jokes on a lily pad,
In this green realm, no one's ever sad!

So come and lay where wild things play,
With laughter echoing every day.
In the shade of trees, life feels so bright,
Where joy is simple, and hearts take flight.

The Grace of Gentle Times

A breeze, a wink from the old oak tree,
As ants throw a dance party, oh so free!
The sun, a golden jellybean,
Winks at clouds that float and preen.

Grass blades gossip beneath the sky,
While butterflies flutter and pass by.
The chipmunks wear their Sunday best,
And even naps become a quest!

The pond reflects the giggles loud,
As frogs leap high, feeling proud.
Fish flip for the latest news,
In a world so silly, they've nothing to lose!

Time lingers here on soft, warm days,
Wrapped in laughter that gently sways.
Nature's rhythm hums a tune,
A merry melody that makes us swoon.

Twilight's Peaceful Song

Evening walks under a silly moon,
Where shadows dance and crickets croon.
The fireflies wear tiny hats,
While owls hoot jokes like friendly spats.

Stars winking like they know a prank,
While night wraps the world in a cozy tank.
A raccoon sneaks by, with snacks galore,
Munching loudly, asking for more!

The breeze tells tales of days gone by,
With whispered laughs, as time flies high.
Each star a wink, each breeze a grin,
Where silliness dwells, no one can win!

So let's laugh through twilight's embrace,
Finding humor in every space.
For life's a joke, a bittersweet song,
And in this moment, we all belong.

Serenity in the Gloaming

As daylight dances into the night,
The clouds wear pajamas, such a sight!
Crickets tune their tiny strings,
While the moon starts giggling, oh what flings!

The fireflies are glowing like tiny stars,
Playing tag with imaginary cars.
The breeze tickles trees with gentle care,
And the world feels lighter, floating in air.

A bear in pajamas sings a soft tune,
While the shadows are making up cartoons.
Silly whispers drift through the trees,
As laughter rides on the wobbly breeze!

So lean back, let the giggles unwind,
In this cozy place, pure joy we find.
As gloaming kisses the day goodbye,
We'll share our laughter under the sky.

Realm of Restfulness

In a land where napkins twirl,
Socks go dancing, flags unfurl.
Clouds wear hats, they sip some tea,
I chuckle softly, feeling free.

Pajama parties at noon's bright hour,
A snooze button's true, unwritten power.
Pillows whisper secrets, oh how divine,
Mice on roller skates, feeling fine.

Serene sandwiches floating on air,
Even the turtles say, 'Don't you dare!'
They laugh at the clock that dares to tick,
In this realm, time's a silly trick.

So, gather your dreams, let worries flee,
In this restful land, you're just so free.
With giggles and grins, we laugh and cheer,
Welcome to the silliness, my dear!

Moonlit Refuge

Underneath the moon's bright gaze,
Silly shadows dance in a haze.
The cat is singing a lullaby,
While rabbits cackle, 'Oh my, oh my!'

Stars are jiving with cosmic flair,
While crickets strum a banjo fair.
The owls hoot jokes, wings flapping wide,
In this refuge, laughter's the guide.

Fireflies twinkle in their best dress,
Announcing a spontaneous fest.
The pond reflects ridiculous dreams,
Of frogs trying out for reality schemes.

With every chuckle, night softly hums,
While playful mischief tickles our thumbs.
Here's to moonlit giggles, light as air,
In this sanctuary, joy's everywhere!

Seraphic Stillness

In a realm where time takes a nap,
Pillows play chess and don a cap.
Daisies wear sunglasses, looking cool,
While clouds draw cartoons by the pool.

Sipping lemonade from a golden cup,
Laughter floats gently as we all sup.
Even the daisies know how to jest,
In this stillness, humor's the best.

Crickets juggling pebbles with glee,
Tell me, what could more fun be?
As butterflies dance to a funny tune,
We all join in under the chuckling moon.

So let's write poems on cotton candy,
In this world of whimsy, soft and handy.
We'll laugh at stillness, giggle at peace,
In seraphic silence, joy will never cease!

Lotus of Ease

On lazy rivers of giggles we row,
Banana boats drift, putting on a show.
The fish flip-flop, avoiding the hook,
While ducks parade with a funny look.

Floating on lily pads, dreams take flight,
Every splash echoes sheer delight.
A turtle in sneakers, racing the breeze,
Challenges frogs, 'Bet you can't tease!'

In the meadow where laughter's the glue,
A snail does stand-up, never shy, 'Boo!'
Bees buzzing jokes in their busy hum,
In leisure's embrace, we all become numb.

So join in the fun, let troubles cease,
In this garden, we plant our peace.
With a wink and a smile, life's a breeze,
Welcome to the world of simple ease!

Moments in the Dappled Light

In the glade where butterflies tease,
Squirrels trade secrets with the trees.
Laughter echoed with every breeze,
While rabbits danced like they owned the keys.

Shadows play games, a silly delight,
Chasing each other, oh what a sight!
Sunbeams tickle, a soft, giddy light,
Even crickets are buzzing with fright.

A turtle is slow, but thinks he's a jet,
Splashing in puddles, he's not done yet.
Blooming flowers smile, a colorful pet,
In this mad world, there's no need to fret.

Blowing bubbles from soap made of dreams,
Tickling the air and bursting at seams.
A giggle escaped from the brook's gentle streams,
In this playground of life, nothing's as it seems.

The Breath of Eternal Calm

A llama named Louie, quite the sight,
Cracks the best jokes, to everyone's delight.
Yelling 'No drama!' while taking a bite,
Of grass that's as fresh as the morning light.

The clouds throw a party, fluffy and wide,
While dandelions dance, no one can hide.
A goat strums a banjo, with so much pride,
Singing of peace, wishing all to abide.

With breezes that tickle and sunrays that play,
Even the flowers join in the ballet.
A butterfly flutters, just here for the day,
Whispers of joy chase the worries away.

As quiet as shadows at dusk sinking low,
A cat on a branch puts on quite the show.
It winks and it purrs, with a cheeky glow,
In this carefree moment, nothing's a woe.

Sanctuary of Serenity

In a park where the squirrels do cheer,
A tortoise nudges, 'Hey, who's over here?'
The birds throw confetti, without any fear,
While flowers giggle, 'Let's get a beer!'

The benches are crowded with wise, old cats,
Discussing the merits of shiny new hats.
A hedgehog jumps in, quite at odds with the spats,
Claiming he's king, while we sit and chat.

Raccoons gather trash, it's their own buffet,
One says, 'At night, we really can play!'
With laughter in pockets, no care for the fray,
In this joyous kingdom, we all want to stay.

A snail makes a throne out of twigs and leaves,
Declaring himself ruler of all that he sees.
While bees buzz with gossip like fluffy, sweet thieves,
In this whimsical space, pure joy we receive.

Whispering Waters

A stream hums a tune, so bubbly and bright,
With fish that wear sunglasses—what a delight!
They wiggle and giggle, in pure frolicking flight,
While frogs host a ball under moon's gentle light.

The reeds sway in rhythm, like dancers so spry,
As dragonflies twirl, aiming high in the sky.
A duck quacks in chorus, oh me, oh my!
With splashes of fun as he flaps nearby.

A picnic unfolds on the soft, green grass,
Where ants throw a party, hoping to pass.
A sandwich was stolen, quite bold for the class,
Yet everyone giggles, as crumbs then amass.

With echoes of laughter, the dusk settles near,
A raccoon sneaks in, to share in the cheer.
The moon beams a smile, and it's perfectly clear,
In this silly wonder, there's nothing to fear.

Where Time Stands Still

In a place where clocks just snooze,
I found my flip-flops and some shoes.
The sunflowers dance without a care,
While I sip lemonade and dare.

The rabbits hold a tea party wide,
Inviting all the squirrels to slide.
I told them jokes, they laughed till they fell,
In this realm, all is well.

The breeze plays tag with my loose hat,
A lazy dog claims a sunny mat.
Time can't tick if it's having fun,
So I stay here—forever young!

With giggles echoing through the trees,
I spot a bubble floating with ease.
Chasing it's a race with my sandwich friend,
But in this bliss, all troubles end.

Embracing the Calm

Sipping tea on my favorite chair,
With my cat who's plotting to snare.
She's not after fish or any mice,
But dreaming of a life of paradise.

The clouds above are cotton candy,
As I nibble on snacks, a bit handy.
My lemonade stands tall like a tower,
I laugh out loud, that's my power.

A breeze whispers secrets so slick,
As a noodle dances, oh what a trick!
The ants join in with a little jig,
Here, the weird just feels big!

With each giggle, my worries depart,
I'm collecting smiles, a true work of art.
So come, please join in my blissful spree,
Where chaos shies away with glee.

Calm Waters Run Clear

The pond reflects the sky like a mirror,
The ducks quack jokes, oh, how they glitter!
I threw in a pebble, causing a splash,
And the fish yelled out, "Hey, don't be rash!"

The turtles chill on a sunken log,
While frogs croak rhythms like a fog.
They hold a concert at noon each day,
With a grand finale—hopping away!

I see a boat sail by, not with a crew,
But with a bear dressed in bright pink too.
He waves his paw, like a screen star,
In this quiet plot, he's gone too far!

So if you're seeking a funny retreat,
Just glide on over; you'll find a seat.
Where laughter floats and worries sink,
In clear calm waters, take a wink!

Hidden Retreat

In the woods where secrets meet,
I found a nest—a cozy seat.
The flowers giggle, the trees all sway,
In this hideout, I'm here to play.

The squirrels play cards, a gamble in style,
With acorn bets that make me smile.
They shout, "You're bluffing!" and snack on fries,
What a wild world with funny ties.

A deer joins in, with shades on tight,
Announcing, "Guess what? I've won the night!"
The moon blinks like a slow signal,
In this hidden spot, life's just sublime.

With each hiccup of laughter and cheer,
I tucked my worries right over here.
So come find me when you need a laugh,
In this secret spot, I'll share the craft.

Echoes of Stillness

In a place where the cactus sings,
And the lizards wear tiny rings,
The sun burns bright, like a golden ace,
But I prefer the shade's cool embrace.

The breeze whispers jokes to the palms,
As squirrels conduct orchestral psalms,
Each chuckle echoes through the sand,
While I search for snacks, that's my grand plan.

A turtle ambles with style so slow,
Winks at the sun, puts on a show,
With watermelons perched as his hat,
He's the sassiest dude, imagine that!

The stars come out with a twinkle and wink,
While I sip juice, deep in thought I sink,
In this absurd place, the laughter flows,
As I ponder the cactus, and its silly toes.

Tranquil Reflections

Where the river giggles and ducks dance,
And frogs in tuxedos take a chance,
The sun's soft rays make the water gleam,
I ponder the life of a milkshake dream.

A fish flips out for a comedic fall,
While a frog croaks out his stand-up call,
The reeds all sway like they're in a band,
In this silly spot, laughter is so grand.

I spotted a snail with a glittery shell,
He waved as if he knew me quite well,
But in a hurry, he dashed off in fright,
Guess my dance moves gave him a fright!

Reflecting on giggles beneath the moon,
I chuckle while listening to the croon,
Of crickets composing a light-hearted tune,
In this tranquil spot, joy fills the room.

Garden of Calm

In a patch where daisies don top hats,
And butterflies tell jokes to the bats,
The sun beaming down, all cozy and bright,
Plants take a nap, oh what a sight!

A hedgehog tries gardening with glee,
But ends up tangled in a vine, oh me!
As roses chuckle at his wild plight,
Their petals shake in pure delight.

Tomatoes are blushing, all ripe and red,
While carrots gossip about what's said,
In whispers of soil, gossip goes round,
"Isn't that cucumber just a clown?"

With laughter in blooms, all things unwind,
In this garden so silly, peace we find,
Nature chuckles, under the sun's balm,
In this humor-filled space, we're ever calm.

Respite from the Storm

When clouds roll in with a grumpy face,
And raindrops come to dance with grace,
A chicken waddles with utmost flair,
As puddles invite her for a splash and stare.

Thunder rumbles like a belly so loud,
Making frogs leap, a jumpy crowd,
While ducks quack jokes to lighten the mood,
In this wacky weather, all seems good.

On the porch, I sip a cup of tea,
Counting raindrops as their number spree,
While the wind plays tunes through the chime,
Nature's theater, a show so sublime.

With lightning flashing like disco lights,
The storm brings laughter in wild delights,
In a wacky tempest, peace is reborn,
As I chuckle beneath the calm after the storm.

Celestial Calm

In a universe so wide and bright,
Stars gather for a comedy night.
Orbiting laughter under moon's glow,
Jokes about gravity steal the show.

Comets zoom by with a wink and a cheer,
Shooting stars shout, 'No worries here!'
Planets roll over, laughing in space,
While aliens giggle, showing their grace.

Galaxies swirl in a dance so absurd,
Every photon a punchline, so absurd!
Black holes shushing, 'Let's keep it down,'
While the universe chuckles, wearing a crown.

So when life gets chaotic, just look above,
Remember the stars and spread the love.
Join in the laughter, it's cosmic and free,
In this non-stop giggle fest, just be!

The Silent Stream

A stream flows quietly, giggling along,
Whispering secrets in a bubbly song.
Fish in tuxedos swim by with grace,
Chasing each other in a slippery race.

Frogs at the banks wear hats of green,
Croaking their jokes, a real funny scene.
The rocks all chuckle, not a word heard,
While turtles nod slowly, spreading the word.

Leaves tumble down like a funny parade,
Each dropping laughing without being afraid.
The dragonflies dance, in a jester's delight,
While the stream carries on, all giggles and light.

So come take a dip in this happy flow,
Where silence is laughter and jokes overflow.
In the stillness, find joy and be keen,
For life's a punchline; it's just a routine!

Abyss of Serenity

In the depths where calmness takes a dive,
Fish tell tales of being alive.
Squid with glasses and octopus arms,
Pop out from the deep with their silly charms.

The coral laughs as the seaweed sways,
While sea urchins roll in a ticklish craze.
Starfish ponder jokes they can't share,
'Cause they just can't comprehend, they swear!

The bubbles emerge like tiny balloons,
Floating up to serenade the tunes.
Even the crabs have a chuckly grin,
As the shark jokes swirl about where they've been.

So dive into depths where giggles may hide,
In the abyss where laughter and joy collide.
Treasures await in the giggly blue,
Where serenity splashes, and life's a zoo!

Gentle Waves of Rest

The waves are gentle, like a soft joke,
Riding the shore, where giggles awoke.
Seagulls cackle, swooping down low,
With silly squawks, they put on a show.

Sandcastles laugh as they puff up with pride,
While the tides tickle them, let's take a ride!
Shells come in, whispering things from the sea,
About fish with mustaches, oh can't you see?

Beach balls bouncing with laughter and zest,
Rolling on by like they're on a quest.
Kids build dreams with popsicle sticks,
As the sun winks, pulling out its tricks.

So close your eyes and feel the tide,
Let the waves sweep you, take you for a ride.
In the gentle laughter of the setting sun,
Rest in the fun where we all are one!

Mirage of Peace

In a desert where camels wear shades,
A pool of lemonade quickly cascades.
Sipping joy from a cactus' embrace,
Life's hiccups turn into a funny race.

Sand castles wobble, then tumble down,
As seashells giggle, wearing a frown.
A mirage shows up with a dancing cat,
Onlookers burst out with a hearty splat!

Under the sun, a towel parade,
Beach balls bouncing; the plans we've made.
Where serenity hides in a peachy treat,
The laughter echoes, isn't life sweet?

With flip-flops flapping, it's quite the scene,
While sunflowers sport their shades of green.
So let's toast to the joy that we find,
In this mirage where calm's unconfined.

Haven of Harmony

In a forest where squirrels wear tiny vests,
And birds with beaks host their feathered quests.
Leaves rustle softly like a whispering mime,
While rabbits breakdance, oh, isn't it prime?

The brook flows past in a giggly stream,
Where fish jump high to fulfill their dream.
A toad in a tux takes the spotlight bright,
With frogs as his backup, a comical sight!

Mushrooms hold meetings, discussing the dew,
While fireflies twinkle — a disco debut!
The trees stretch their branches in a graceful sway,
In this haven of giggles, we swing and we play.

So come take a break from the hustle and fuss,
Join this fiesta of fun, it's a must!
Harmony dances with laughter and cheers,
In this whimsical world that banishes fears.

Solace in the Silence

In a library where books wear thick glasses,
And giggling critics sneak glances at classes.
A mouse spins tales of his perilous cheese,
While pages flip gently in a friendly breeze.

Tea parties held by literary mice,
Discussing their plots while rolling the dice.
A quill that quakes when it writes a new tale,
As echoes of laughter drift far down the trail.

The chairs hum a tune, quite off-key to the ear,
While shadows convene for their annual cheer.
In this silence, silliness softly bloats,
As wordplay ambushes and mischief promotes.

Oh, solitude reigns with a side of delight,
As characters frolic both day and the night.
In the stillness we find, with a chuckle so grand,
Life's little joys just waiting at hand.

Elysian Fields of Rest

Where sugar plums dance in cotton candy sky,
Clouds wearing helmets that float quickly by.
Kites made of laughter soar high on a breeze,
While butterflies twiddle, adopting a tease.

Beneath the sun's giggle, the grass has a play,
As ants march in formation, making their way.
Each flower tells jokes in a funny bouquet,
Where dreams trod softly in a jolly array.

Picnics explode with delight at each bite,
While laughter plays tag with a squirrel in flight.
A napkin's caught dancing, a wild serenade,
Its humor contagious, no moments to fade.

In these fields of cheer, where silliness reigns,
Joy sprouts like daisies, escaping the chains.
So let's lay back and embrace the fresh zest,
In laughter and light, we find our true rest.

Veil of Peace

In a world where silence reigns,
I found a rug with magic stains.
It tells jokes with a squeaky voice,
And makes me giggle, oh what a choice!

I sip tea from a mug that sings,
As birds wear hats and do funny flings.
Laughter bubbles like an old creek,
In this calm place, I can't help but geek.

When the breeze whispers, it tickles my ear,
And trees dance with joy, spreading good cheer.
Clouds wear sunglasses, lounging in style,
While I lie back and grin for a while.

A hammock that bounces, a duck on a skateboard,
In my little world, absurdity is adored.
Soft giggles float up with the sun's gentle light,
In this peaceful land, every day feels just right.

The Quiet Corner

In the quiet nook, you'll find a chair,
That whispers secrets with plenty of flair.
It tells puns about cats in a sweet, soft tone,
While my coffee cup mimics a babbling stone.

A lizard in sunglasses dances by,
And a squirrel gives me the wink of an eye.
Each tick of the clock makes a silly sound,
As the cushions come alive and spin around.

The floor is a map of wiggly dreams,
Where nothing is serious, or so it seems.
A mouse on a skateboard zooms past my toes,
And tickles my feet with its tiny little nose.

In this haven of joy, where laughter is bright,
Even shadows join in the light-hearted fight.
With each giggle, I feel more at ease,
In this cozy corner, I'm happy to freeze.

Oasis of the Mind

In the haven where thoughts gently flow,
The brain's on a joyride, don't be too slow!
Thoughts wearing hats are doing the cha-cha,
While giggles leap high like a wild little llama.

I sip from a cup that bursts into song,
And my pen starts to dance, oh, doesn't it belong?
Clouds twirl around, playing peek-a-boo,
As my ideas float by like an old shoe.

The calmness wraps round me like a warm hug,
While my worries play hide-and-seek with a bug.
A gentle breeze juggles knock-knock jokes,
While I grin at my thoughts like happy, silly folks.

In this repose, where light-hearted wins,
Even the shadows are ready to spin.
With each chuckle, my mind takes flight,
In this tranquil space, everything feels right.

Tranquility's Touch

In a calm spot where giggles bloom wide,
I found a snail wearing a slip-and-slide.
It bravely zooms past, doesn't seem to care,
While squirrels debate who has the best hair.

A waterfall chuckles, it's not feeling shy,
As leaves fall like feathers from a sky-high pie.
Butterflies wearing capes dodge all the fuss,
And the flowers play cards in colorful gusts.

The grass tickles toes with a mischievous grin,
While tiny ants plan a city to win.
Every soft whisper becomes a good joke,
And clouds join in too, turning all into smoke.

With each Lord of Laughs, the moments unfold,
Where nothing is serious, just tales to be told.
In this peaceful nest, oh do let me stay,
With laughter as sunlight radiating the day.

Pathway to Peace

With shoes untied and socks a mess,
I stroll along this path, I guess.
Birds chirp tunes of silly delight,
While squirrels dance in playful flight.

The flowers giggle, such vibrant hues,
They tickle my nose, oh what a ruse!
I trip on daisies, land on the grass,
Laughing at nature, oh, what a class!

The sun winks down, a cheeky grin,
A warm embrace, where fun begins.
Waves of laughter float through the trees,
In this joyous moment, I feel the breeze.

I close my eyes, let worries drop,
In this silly scene, I leap and hop.
With giggles and grins, I find my space,
On this path, it's a silly race!

Soft Rays of Rest

Soft rays peek through curtains wide,
With sleepy giggles, I can't abide.
Pillows puffed like clouds in flight,
Teddy bears plotting a frolic night.

The blanket fort smiles, sturdy and bold,
Whispers of dreams, both spicy and old.
A hammock swings, a canvas of cheer,
While dust bunnies dance without a fear.

Footsteps and muffles from downstairs roam,
As Mom sings loudly, 'You can't just moan!'
The pet goldfish joins in with a splash,
Together we giggle and make quite the dash.

So here I lay, with laughter and rest,
Soft rays surrounding, feeling so blessed.
In this silly refuge, the world seems bright,
A kingdom of coziness, pure delight!

Secret Garden of Calm

Behind the hedge, where wild things grow,
A garden of secrets, funny to know.
The tomatoes chuckle and tease the peas,
While raindrops laugh from the swaying trees.

A worm in sunglasses takes a slow crawl,
He tips his hat, and I can't help but sprawl.
Butterflies flutter, like pieces of mail,
Delivering giggles on the soft breeze trail.

The gnomes out here play poker at dusk,
With cabbage leaves as chips, it's a must!
They wink and nod, so slyly they play,
While I sneak closer, trying not to sway.

In my closet, I hide a squeal,
For this garden of giggles makes joy feel real.
Amongst the sillies, I find my charm,
As nature's laughter does keep me warm!

Gentle Breeze

A gentle breeze tickles my ear,
With whispers of laughter, I can hear.
It twirls my hair like a playful dance,
Inviting me out for a silly chance.

The trees sway palms, in jolly embrace,
As branches high-five, a charming race.
Leaves giggle softly, a rustling sound,
In this midst of joy, pure whimsy found.

Frogs croak puns from their lily-pad stage,
While ants march on like a funny parade.
Clouds ride by on a joke-telling spree,
I laugh out loud, feeling so free.

With each gentle push, the world's a delight,
I chase after chuckles, wearing pure light.
In this playful breeze, no worries are found,
A treasure of laughter, so joyfully bound!

Clarity Amidst the Whispers

In a land where silence struts,
Even squirrels hold their butts.
The breeze whispers a silly song,
As the trees giggle all day long.

Clouds float by like silly sheep,
While crickets dance in rhythmic leap.
A frog croaks jokes about the rain,
And all complaints are just plain vain.

Sunbeams play hide-and-seek,
With shadows laughably cheek to cheek.
Here, even the rocks crack a grin,
As the laughter flows from within.

So take a seat on a comfy stone,
Join the chatter, don't feel alone.
In this place where humor thrives,
Laughter is what truly survives.

Surrender to Stillness

Fish in ponds wear tiny hats,
While turtles spin tales like old bats.
The reeds sway in comedic flair,
As ducks gossip without a care.

A snail races with a slow crawl,
Cheering on his friends from the wall.
The butterflies flutter, wings of delight,
Trading jests beneath the moonlight.

Every whisper is a playful tease,
Encouraging laughter in the sweetest breeze.
Gravity, it seems, has lost its hold,
As giggles and joy are spun into gold.

So let your worries float away,
Join the antics that come out to play.
In this stillness with a chuckling twist,
You'll find peace wrapped in a humorous mist.

A Realm of Soft Glow

Stars twinkle like riddles untold,
Each one a secret, but oh so bold.
The moon grins wide with a knowing jest,
Glowing softly, it's truly the best.

Fireflies wear tiny glow-in-the-dark shoes,
They flash disco lights, singing the blues.
A nightingale croons to the rhythm of cheer,
As laughter dances and draws us near.

Silhouettes of trees sway in delight,
Sharing tales of the day and its slight.
Laughter bubbles from the brook so clear,
In this soft glow, there's nothing to fear.

So come gather 'round, let your spirit soar,
In this realm where joy is never a chore.
With each twinkle, a story set free,
It's where all of us just want to be.

Pages of a Calm Afterlife

In the library of laughter divine,
Books chuckle softly with stories to pine.
Each page turns with a giggle and spin,
Where wisdom and humor team up to win.

The chairs take bets on who'll read next,
While the table of sages gets quite perplexed.
A tale of a cat with a wizard's hat,
Leaves us gasping, "Imagine that!"

Scrolls of joy are tucked away neat,
Each line a tickle, so silly and sweet.
In this calm, wisdom wears funny clothes,
And the heart overflows as laughter grows.

So if you seek joy beyond this vie,
Join the chapters that make you sigh.
With every laugh, a page turns anew,
In this calm afterlife, we'll welcome you too.

Whispers of the Serene

In a land where chickens wear shades,
And cats begin to serenade,
The clouds float by, like lazy sheep,
While frogs in bow ties try to leap.

A squirrel juggles acorns with flair,
While turtles race without a care,
The sun winks down, a playful tease,
As bees do ballet, buzzing with ease.

Bubbles float on a gentle breeze,
Where hippos pirouette with such ease,
Each leaf a note in nature's song,
In this odd place, nothing feels wrong.

So come and join, don't be late,
For laughter here is truly great,
In a park where giggles never cease,
And everything's a bit of a tease.

The Still Waters' Embrace

Where ducks wear hats and swim with grace,
And fish pop up to join the race,
The waters shimmer, a silly sight,
As frogs jump in, their socks turned bright.

A turtle tells jokes, slow as can be,
While dragonflies dance, just wait and see,
The sun sets low, a golden hue,
As crickets strum to the evening's view.

With every splash, a raucous cheer,
The laughter echoes far and near,
In this calm spot, all things collide,
Where fun and joy meet side by side.

So let your worries float away,
In this carefree place, come what may,
For even fish can grin with glee,
In waters where laughter roams free.

Sanctuary of Silence

In a grove where silence cracks a grin,
And squirrels plot their next big win,
The shadows giggle as they sway,
As trees play hide and seek all day.

A hedgehog in specs reads a book,
While wise old owls just take a look,
The breeze whispers secrets to the air,
And starlings practice their wild flair.

Beneath the boughs, the world goes mute,
With dancing leaves, no need for loot,
Here laughter grows in hidden spots,
As nature spins the best of plots.

So find your peace, and take a chance,
Join the woodland's merry dance,
Where stillness sings, and smiles abound,
In this calm nook, joy is found.

Beneath the Canopy of Calm

Beneath the trees where shadows play,
A parrot tells jokes, bright and gay,
With every chuckle from a frog,
The turtles sit and nod in fog.

A sleepy sloth once took a nap,
But woke to find a nearby chap,
Who wore a crown made out of cheese,
And said, 'Life's too short—let's just squeeze!'

With sun on leaves, a golden show,
The river sparkles, soft and slow,
While ants in shades parade along,
As trees join in this jolly song.

So here we'll laugh, and life's a breeze,
In this strange place where hearts can tease,
For in this haven, joy takes flight,
Beneath the canopy, everything's bright.

Tranquil Essence

In a sandy spot, a llama sips,
Donning shades, it strikes cool flips.
Palm trees wave, gossiping with glee,
While turtles attempt to dance like me.

Cacti wear hats, the party's alive,
With chubby iguanas discussing their drive.
Lizards start rapping with utmost flair,
As a nearby rabbit sings without a care.

Clouds drift by, puffed like cotton candy,
Sipping soda, feeling quite dandy.
The breeze plays tunes on leaves so bright,
Making the sun bathe us in laughter's light.

Here every chuckle turns into a cheer,
Where giggles are served like lemonade beer.
In this sandy dream, pure joy does bloom,
With a llama's soft laugh echoing the room.

The Silent Sanctuary

An owl in a jacket, all dressed to impress,
Conducting a choir of frogs, no less.
The trees are all nodding, it's quite the sight,
As fireflies buzz in synchronized flight.

A sloth in a hammock taking a snooze,
Says, 'Life's too quick, you gotta just cruise!'
The branches make whispers, amusing the crowd,
As squirrels crack jokes, all drawing a crowd.

Even the raccoons steal glances with glee,
Grabbing popcorn, excited as can be.
The stars are like winks, oh, how they shine,
As we gather for tales 'round the moonlit dine.

It's a place where the giggle turns into a song,
In the quietest spots, mischief belongs.
Gather your friends, all bizarre and uncanny,
In the silent haven, let laughter be plenty.

Whisper of the Leaves

Leaves rustle secrets, oh what a tease,
As squirrels play poker with infinite ease.
A rabbit juggles, a dance on the ground,
While the bushes all giggle, no silence found.

The breeze tells tickles, the sun makes a pun,
With shadows that dither, just having some fun.
A cat naps nearby, dreaming of fish,
While ants form a band, aiming to swish.

Trees share tall tales of their wives in bloom,
While silly old owls send hoots through the room.
Underneath the green, cheer's never at bay,
Where whispers turn wild in the light of day.

In this leafy abode, where laughter's the goal,
Each fumble and mumble enhances the soul.
Join in the jest where the fun never leaves,
And submerge in the laughter the treetops believe.

A Quietude Dance

In a meadow so bright, bears waltz on the grass,
Two flamingos in tutus make quite the sass.
With gentle hops, the rabbits join in,
While the sun beams down, tempting a grin.

The wind shakes its hips, a rhythmic delight,
As the daisies do spin, colors popping just right.
A hedgehog moonwalks, feeling so spry,
With a band of crickets crooning nearby.

A worm does a twist, oh, how it grooves,
While the butterflies flutter, showing their moves.
A dancing parade in the sun's warm embrace,
Where each little laugh is a joyful showcase.

In the hush of the woodlands, fun takes the lead,
With nonsense galore, it plants the best seed.
So sway with the rhythm, let laughter enhance,
For life's a grand stage, just join in the dance!

Shadows of Serenity

In the park where shadows dance,
Lemons try to cosplay as ants.
A frog leaps, thinking he's a star,
While squirrels plot, and laugh from afar.

Breeze whispers jokes, a tickle to hear,
As clouds wear hats, oh how they cheer!
A quiet cat joins in the fun,
With a paw on a laptop, he can't be outdone.

Still Waters Run Deep

Puddles reflect a wiggly worm,
Who struts around, with flair and charm.
Even the ducks are in on the game,
Quacking funny lines, earning their fame.

A fish makes a splash, trying to dance,
While lily pads laugh, oh what a chance!
A turtle gets stuck in his own little shell,
Screaming for help, though all is well.

Meadow of Moments

In the meadow where daisies play,
Butterflies crack jokes in the bright sunray.
A rabbit throws a party, oh what a sight,
With carrots on the table, it's pure delight.

Grasshoppers sigh, tired from their leaps,
While a sleeping mole has funny dreams in heaps.
The wind tells stories that tickle your toes,
As everyone giggles, no one quite knows.

A Breath of Calm

An umbrella spins, caught by the breeze,
While bees hold a meeting under the trees.
A frog in a bow tie sings a sweet tune,
Inviting all passersby, on a bright afternoon.

A snail in shades glides at a slow speed,
While ants make a line, just taking the lead.
With laughter and joy, the calm does abide,
In the quirkiest moments, let happiness ride.

www.ingramcontent.com/pod-product-compliance
Lightning Source LLC
Chambersburg PA
CBHW072217070526
44585CB00015B/1379